HOCKEY

by Jonatha A. Brown
Reading consultant: Susan Nations, M.Ed., author/literacy coach/consultant

WEEKLY WR READER®
EARLY LEARNING LIBRARY

Please visit our web site at: www.earlyliteracy.cc
For a free color catalog describing Weekly Reader® Early Learning Library's list of high-quality books, call 1-877-445-5824 (USA) or 1-800-387-3178 (Canada).
Weekly Reader® Early Learning Library's fax: (414) 336-0164.

Library of Congress Cataloging-in-Publication Data

Brown, Jonatha A.
    Hockey / Jonatha A. Brown.
      p. cm. — (My favorite sport)
      Includes bibliographical references and index.
      ISBN 0-8368-4340-1 (lib. bdg.)
      ISBN 0-8368-4347-9 (softcover)
      1. Hockey —Juvenile literature. I. Title.
    GV847.25.B76   2004
    796.962—dc22   2004041978

This edition first published in 2005 by
Weekly Reader® Early Learning Library
330 West Olive Street, Suite 100
Milwaukee, WI 53212 USA

Editor: JoAnn Early Macken
Art direction, cover and layout design: Tammy West
Photo research: Diane Laska-Swanke

Photo credits: Cover, title, p. 10, Gregg Andersen; p. 5 © Hulton Archive/Getty Images;
p. 7 Tammy West/© Weekly Reader Early Learning Library, 2005; pp. 8, 9 © Jim Rogash/
WireImage.com; pp. 12, 16 © Bob Levey/WireImage.com; p. 13 © Bruce Bennett Studios/BBS/
WireImage.com; p. 14 © Glenn Cratty/Getty Images; p. 15 © Brian Bahr/Getty Images; p. 17
© Elsa/Getty Images; p. 18 © Chris Cole/Getty Images; p. 20 © Harry How/Getty Images; p. 21
© Matthew Stockman/Getty Images

Printed in the United States of America

1 2 3 4 5 6 7 8 9 08 07 06 05 04

Table of Contents

CHAPTER 1

Hockey Then and Now

Ice hockey started in Canada during the 1800s. It probably came from stick-and-ball games played by Native Americans. Some rules came from lacrosse. Others came from games similar to field hockey.

Canadian teams formed the National Hockey League (NHL) in 1917. Soon U.S. teams joined the NHL. Players in the NHL are pros.

Hockey has been the most popular sport in Canada for a long time. It is also very popular in the United States and other parts of the world. The Olympic Games include hockey for men's and women's teams.

Hockey probably came from stick-and-ball games played by Native people.

CHAPTER 2

Hockey Basics

In hockey, two teams play against each other on a long ice skating rink. At each end of the rink is a goal. The goal is a metal frame with net around three sides. The front of the goal is open.

All players wear ice skates. They also carry hockey sticks. They use the sticks to hit the puck — a small, thick piece of hard rubber. Each team tries to shoot the puck into the other team's net to score a goal.

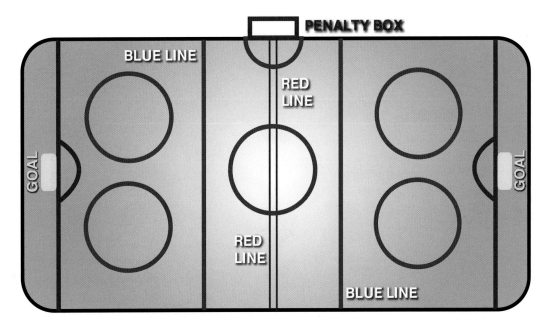

Each team has six players. One is the goalie. The goalie protects his or her team's goal. Two defensemen help the goalie. They all try to keep the other team from scoring.

Harvard University's goalie focuses on the action as she protects her team's goal.

A forward playing for St. Lawrence University chases after the puck. A Harvard defender tries to stop her.

The other three players on each team are forwards. Their main job is to score. They pass the puck back and forth until one of them has a good shot at the other team's goal.

Both teams fight for control of the puck and try to score goals. Each goal counts as one point. At the end of the game, the team with the most points wins. If the teams are tied when the game ends, it can go into overtime.

Two young players face off to begin play. Each will try to control the puck after it is dropped.

CHAPTER 3

Exciting Plays

Hockey is a fast-paced game. The puck is almost always moving. Players zoom back and forth as they defend their goal and try to score. Every minute of a game can be exciting.

Action is fast and furious in front of the goal. Here, the goalie is covered by ice chips as the puck sails over the net.

Play gets really fierce when the puck is near a team's goal. Often several players are scrambling for the puck just in front of the net. The fans are on the edge of their seats. Will the attackers score? Will the other team fight them off? Will the goalie make a big save? It is a tense moment for players and fans alike!

The game can be just as exciting when the action takes place away from the goal. A forward sees an opening. He clobbers the puck. It slices through the air and whizzes past the other players. The goalie tries to stop it, but the puck slams into the net. Goal! The forward scores with a slap shot.

Wayne Gretzky, known to NHL fans as "The Great One," unleashes one of his mighty slap shots.

U.S. goalie Mike Richter makes a save against Claude Lemieux of Canada on a breakaway during the World Cup of Hockey.

Sometimes the players are fighting for the puck at one end of the rink. A player breaks away from the pack. He charges down the ice alone. He pushes the puck ahead of him with his stick. Now he is facing only one foe — the goalie. Will he score, or will the goalie make a great save?

A good defense provides lots of excitement, too. Goalies often make great saves. They use their sticks to stop the puck. They catch it in their gloves. They block it with their skates or their bodies. They do whatever they can to stop the puck! Then they dump it onto an empty patch of ice, away from the goal.

This goalie has made a save with his helmet!

Houston and Cincinnati players mix it up during an American Hockey League playoff game. Someone will be spending time in the box!

Hockey is a rough sport. But it has rules against certain kinds of rough play. A player who commits a foul gets a penalty. He must sit in the penalty box. Most penalties last two minutes. While the player is in the box, the other team has "the power play." This means that they have more players on the ice. Many teams use the power play to score goals.

Some of hockey's most exciting moments come after the regular game has ended. When a game ends in a tie, it can go into overtime. In overtime, a single goal can decide the game.

The action on the boards is rough, but the fans seem to be enjoying it!

Save! The goalie is on his back. But he has kept the puck out of the net during this shoot-out in the Olympics.

What if overtime ends and the score is still tied? When this happens, a shoot-out can decide who wins. In a shoot-out, one player at a time takes a shot at the goal. The goalie tries to block the shot. The two teams take turns. When one team scores during a round and the other does not, the scoring team wins.

CHAPTER 4

Championship Hockey

Every hockey league has its own championship playoff series. In Canada, for example, the Abby Hoffman Cup is awarded to the nation's top women's team.

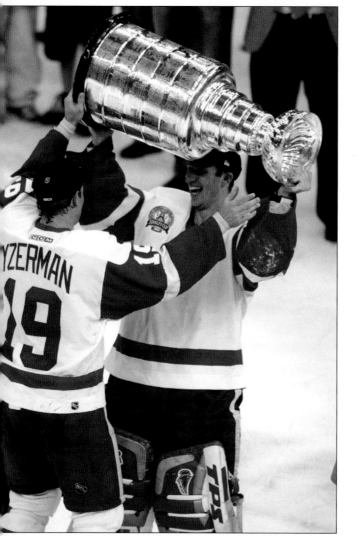

The Stanley Cup is the most famous hockey trophy in North America. Each year, the top two teams in the National Hockey League compete for it.

Members of the Detroit Red Wings celebrate their victory in the NHL Stanley Cup finals.

Some of the most exciting, most famous hockey games have been played at the Olympics. These games draw more fans than almost any other Olympic sport. The top men's and women's teams win gold medals. They often come home as sports heroes!

"We're Number One!" Members of the U.S. women's team celebrate a victory in the Winter Olympics.

Glossary

defensemen – players who usually stay back toward the goal and help the goalie keep the other team from scoring

penalty – a punishment for committing a foul or breaking a rule

power play – an attack made by a team that has all of its players on the ice against a team that has fewer players because of penalties

pros (short for professionals) – people who play sports as a paid job

trophy – a prize given to a winner in sports

For More Information

Books

Defensemen. Hockey's Hottest (series). James Duplacey (Kids Can Press)

Hockey Rules! The Official Illustrated Kids' Guide to the NHL Rules and Regulations. Dan Diamond (Somerville House USA)

Ice Hockey. Jack Otten (PowerKids Press)

The Magic Hockey Stick. Peter Maloney and Felicia Zekauskas (Dial)

Z Is for Zamboni: A Hockey Alphabet. Matt M. Napier (Gale Group)

Web Sites

NHL.com for Kids
nhl.com/kids/index.html?clk=001
Schedules, games, and contests
The Science of Hockey
www.exploratorium.edu/hockey/
Learn about ice, skating, shooting, and more

Index

About the Author

Jonatha A. Brown has been writing children's books since leaving a corporate position in 2001. She holds a B.A. in English from St. Lawrence University in Canton, New York. Jonny lives in Phoenix, Arizona, where she is a fan of the Arizona Diamondbacks. Her favorite sport is dressage.